FABULOUS
Bake Sale
& Gift
Recipes

C0-CEC-505

KÖNEMANN

Pretty Packaging

Eye-catching presentation will boost proceeds at your next bake sale, and adds a delightful personal touch to gift-giving.

The most attractive packaging is often the simplest: colorful wrapping paper with striking ribbons, or a theme created around the seaside or the garden. Inexpensive items and recyclable materials—old jars and bottles, brown paper and cardboard, flowers, shells, fabric, paper ribbon and doilies, raffia and interesting containers—can all be combined with wonderful effects.

Wrapping paper in a variety of colors and textures is the easiest way to package most items. Use brilliant shades of tissue paper, clear or colored cellophane, or handmade papers. Even newspaper you were going to toss in the trash can be used imaginatively. Brown paper looks effective tied bon-bon style around candies and secured with colored jute or ribbon.

Personalize your wrapping paper: cover heavy paper with potato prints; spray with metallic and colored paints for a dappled effect; stencil, or decorate with stickers.

Try using crushed brown paper instead of the usual fabric jar covers; wind string over the top to create the look of a parcel and finish with a string tassel. To make the tassel, cut eight or ten similar lengths of string, knot together at the center, then fold in half at this point and tie the lengths together again slightly lower than the top knot. Clip the base of the tassel so threads are the same length; tie to the jar with a string bow.

Paper doilies make ideal covers for jars. Use them to line boxes or plates, painted or plain, or use as a stencil.

Position the doily on the surface you wish to stencil (paper or fabric). Apply paint with a stencil brush, or spray it on. Allow to dry before lifting the doily.

Crepe paper is a old decorating favorite—the bright colors and the texture help create

a sense of festivity. Use to make small bags. Cut square or rectangular shapes the same size from crepe paper, fold in half (lengthways if rectangular) and punch holes at even intervals along each side. Cut thin strips of crepe paper and thread through the holes, knotting at each end. Insert items that you wish to wrap and tie at the top with ribbon.

Bottles come in interesting shapes and colors. Dress-up a bottle of herb vinegar with a raffia bow tied around the neck or handle.

Old boxes can be re-used: paint them, cover with paper or festoon with ribbons. Take the bottom half of a flat box, punch holes through the corners and tie with bows to make a pretty presentation box for cookies and candies.

Purchase patterned, papier-maché or glossy gift boxes and individualize them with some colorful fabric lining in interesting textures; trim with braid or ribbon.

Terracotta pots and trays, bowls and baskets make lovely containers for food. A fruit cake, cookies or candies will look great in a large pot wrapped in clear cellophane and finished with ribbon or colored string. An inexpensive dish towel is a perfect wrapping for homemade muffins.

Create a seaside theme by wrapping boxes and jars in handmade paper or calico, then tying or knotting rope around them. Attach shells and other beach paraphernalia with glue and tape, or secure them beneath the rope.

To finish, raffia, rope and paper ribbon combine well with natural and brown papers, calico and muslin. Form wired ribbons in different widths, patterns and colors into cascading lengths or full bows. Preserved fruit slices, citrus peel strips, and fresh grapes or berries look great on top of jars, or use fresh or dried flowers. Attach cardboard or thick paper gift tags.

Use shells, flowers, leaves, fabric, cardboard, interesting bottles and jars, and a dash of imagination to dress up your gifts.

Cakes & Cookies

Traditional favorites or something a little different, home-baked goodies like these are sure to tempt them at the cake stall. Pack them in attractive boxes or colorful wrapping to make wonderful gifts.

Blueberry Muffins

Preparation time:
  20 minutes
Total cooking time:
  15–20 minutes
Makes 14

2 cups all-purpose
  flour
2¹/2 teaspoons baking
  powder
¹/4 teaspoon baking
  soda
pinch salt
²/3 cup sugar
1–2 teaspoons grated
  lemon rind
1 cup fresh blueberries
1 egg
1 cup milk
3 oz butter, melted

1. Preheat oven to moderate 350°F. Brush fourteen ¹/3-cup capacity muffin cups with oil or melted butter. Place combined sifted flour, baking powder, soda and salt into a large bowl. Add sugar and rind; mix well. Stir in blueberries.
2. Whisk together egg, milk and cooled melted butter in a large jug. Pour onto dry ingredients; using large metal spoon, mix until just combined.
3. Spoon into muffin cups until ²/3 full. Bake for 15–20 minutes or until muffins have risen and are lightly browned, and until a skewer comes out clean when inserted in center. Leave in pans for 3–5 minutes before placing on wire racks to cool.

> HINT
> If using frozen berries, add at the last minute, while still frozen. Fresh or frozen raspberries may also be used. Cooled muffins may be iced with a thin lemon icing.

Blueberry Muffins (top) and Family Chocolate Cake

Family Chocolate Cake

Preparation time:
  15 minutes
Total cooking time:
  50 minutes
Makes one 8 inch round cake

1 1/2 cups self-rising
  flour
1/2 cup cocoa powder
1 cup sugar
6 1/2 oz plain yogurt
2 eggs
6 1/2 oz butter, melted
1 3/4 oz dark chocolate,
  grated

Icing
1 3/4 oz dark chocolate,
  chopped
1 3/4 oz butter
1/2 cup confectioners'
  sugar
1–2 tablespoons yogurt
  or sour cream

1. Preheat oven to moderate 350°F. Brush a deep 8 inch pan with oil or melted butter; line base and sides with waxed paper; grease paper.
2. Place flour, cocoa powder and sugar into food processor. Add yogurt, eggs and butter. Using the pulse action, process for 15 seconds or until mixture is smooth. Add grated chocolate and process until ingredients are combined.
3. Pour mixture into prepared pan; smooth the surface. Bake for 50 minutes or until a skewer comes out clean when inserted into the center of cake.
4. Stand cake in pan for 10 minutes before turning onto a wire rack to cool.
5. *To make Icing:* Place chocolate in small heatproof bowl. Stand bowl over a pan of simmering water and stir until chocolate has melted; remove from heat. Beat butter and confectioners' sugar with electric beaters in small bowl until smooth and creamy. Add chocolate and yogurt or sour cream; beat well until combined. Spread evenly over top of cake using a palette knife. Decorate top with whole, fresh strawberries, if you like.

HINT
Take care when melting chocolate to prevent any moisture coming into contact with the chocolate. If this happens the chocolate may become a rough, unworkable mass.

Chewy Muesli Bars

Preparation time:
  10 minutes
Total cooking time:
  45 minutes
Makes 24 bars

4 oz unsalted butter
1/2 cup sugar
1/2 cup light brown
  sugar, lightly packed
2 tablespoons honey
3 1/2 cups untoasted
  muesli
3/4 cup shredded
  coconut
1 teaspoon ground
  cinnamon
1/2 cup glacé cherries,
  chopped
1/2 cup golden raisins
1/2 cup currants

1. Preheat oven to moderately slow 315°F. Brush a 12 x 8 inch rectangular pan with oil or melted butter. Line base and sides with waxed paper; grease paper.
2. Combine butter, sugars and honey in a pan. Stir over low heat until sugar has dissolved and butter has melted. Remove from heat.
3. Combine muesli, coconut, cinnamon, cherries, golden raisins and currants in a bowl. Make a well in center. Pour butter mixture onto dry ingredients;

Chewy Muesli Bars

combine thoroughly.
4. Press the mixture firmly into prepared pan. Using a sharp knife, mark top of cake into 24 equal bars. Bake for 35 minutes, reduce oven temperature to very slow 250°F and cook for another 10 minutes. Leave cake in pan for 15 minutes before turning onto a board to cool. Cut into bars when completely cold.

Store Muesli Bars in an airtight container in the refrigerator for up to one week.

Note: Pipe a pattern in melted chocolate to decorate, if you like.

Shortbread

Preparation time:
  20 minutes + 30
  minutes refrigeration
Total cooking time:
  25 minutes
Makes 2 shortbread

8 oz butter, chopped
$^1/_2$ teaspoon vanilla
  extract
$^3/_4$ cup confectioners'
  sugar
2 cups all-purpose flour
$^1/_2$ cup rice flour

1. Preheat oven to
moderate 350°F. Line
two baking sheets
with waxed paper.
2. Using electric beaters,
beat butter and vanilla
in small bowl until light
and creamy. Transfer to
large bowl. Add sifted
confectioners' sugar,
beat another minute.
3. Using a wooden
spoon, fold in sifted
flours a spoonful at a
time; mix well. Place
dough in refrigerator
for 30 minutes until
firm. Divide dough into
two portions. Flatten
slightly, then roll each
into a circle, between
two sheets of waxed
paper, to a thickness
of $^1/_4$ inch. Carefully
transfer to baking sheets.
4. Crimp circle edges
with fingers, or use a
fork. Prick all over with
a skewer. Score across
each circle to mark out

8 wedges. Bake 20–25
minutes, or until golden
and crisp. Cut into
wedges along score
lines. Transfer to wire
rack while still warm;
leave to cool.

Dark Ginger and Molasses Cake

Preparation time:
  30 minutes
Total cooking time:
  50–60 minutes
*Makes one 9 inch
bundt cake*

fine stale bread crumbs
  or corn flake crumbs
4 oz butter, softened
$^1/_2$ cup light brown
  sugar
$^1/_3$ cup black molasses
3 eggs
2 cups all-purpose
  flour
1 teaspoon baking soda
2 teaspoons ground
  cloves
1 teaspoon ground
  cinnamon
1 teaspoon ground
  ginger
$^2/_3$ cup sour cream
$3^1/_2$ oz preserved
  ginger, finely chopped
  and including syrup,
  or $^1/_2$ cup chunky
  ginger conserve

Lemon Glaze
$^2/_3$ cup confectioners'
  sugar
1–2 tablespoons lemon
  juice
$1^3/_4$ oz butter, softened

1. Preheat oven to
moderately slow 315°F.
Brush a round 9 inch
deep ring or bundt pan
with oil or melted butter;
coat pan with bread or
corn flake crumbs.
2. Beat butter and sugar
with electric beaters
until light and creamy.
Beat in molasses.
3. Add eggs gradually,
beating well after each
addition. Using a metal
spoon, fold in the sifted
flour, baking soda and
spices with sour cream.
Fold in chopped ginger
and syrup or conserve.
4. Spoon into prepared
pan; smooth the surface.
Bake 50–60 minutes,
or until a fine skewer
comes out clean when
inserted in center. Leave
in pan 10 minutes
before turning onto a
wire rack to cool.
To make Lemon Glaze:
Combine confectioners'
sugar, juice and butter
in a small heatproof
bowl. Stand bowl over a
pan of simmering water
and stir until smooth.
Remove from heat,
brush over warm cake.
Decorate with candied
orange peel and fresh
strawberries, if you like.

Dark Ginger & Molasses Cake (top) and Shortbread

Panforte

Preparation time:
 30 minutes
Total cooking time:
 40 minutes
*Makes two 9 inch
square or round cakes*

8 oz almonds
8 oz hazelnuts
1¹/2 lb mixed dried
 fruits: seeded raisins,
 pitted prunes, pitted
 dates, soft dried figs,
 mixed candied citrus
 peel
2 cups all-purpose flour
1 tablespoon pumpkin
 pie spice
1 tablespoon ground
 cinnamon
1¹/4 cups sugar
1 cup honey
confectioners' sugar, for
 dusting

1. Preheat oven to
315°F. Brush two
9 inch shallow round
or square cake pans
with melted butter or
oil. Line base and sides
with waxed paper.
2. Place almonds and
hazelnuts on a baking
sheet. Roast in oven for
8–10 minutes, or until
hazelnut skins start to
peel. Remove from
oven. Lower oven heat
to moderately slow
315°F. Wrap hazelnuts
in a cloth and rub
vigorously to remove the
skins. Place whole nuts
in a large mixing bowl.

3. Chop the dried fruit
roughly and add to
bowl. Sift flour and
spices over fruit in bowl.
4. Place sugar and honey
in small pan. Stir over
low heat until sugar has
melted and mixture is
smooth. Bring to boil,
reduce heat and simmer
for about 10–15 minutes
or until syrup reaches
240°F–250°F on a sugar
thermometer (immerse
the bulb of the
thermometer in the syrup
after it has come to the
boil), or a teaspoon of
syrup forms a soft ball
when dropped into a
bowl of iced water. Add
syrup to fruit and flour
in bowl. Using a large
metal spoon, stir until
well combined—mixture
will be stiff.
5. Spoon mixture evenly
into prepared pans.
Flatten with wet hands—
mixture should be
approximately ³/4 inch
deep. Bake 40 minutes.
Leave in pan on wire
rack to cool.
6. When cake is cool,
remove from pan; peel
off waxed paper. Wrap
in plastic wrap and then
in foil. Refrigerate,
or store in a cool, dry
place, until needed.
(Texture and flavor of
cake will improve with
keeping.) Serve, dusted
with confectioners'
sugar, cut into very thin
slices or small squares.

Chocolate Brownies

Preparation time:
 20 minutes
Total cooking time:
 35–40 minutes
Makes 16 squares

5¹/2 oz dark chocolate,
 chopped
4 oz butter
2 eggs, lightly beaten
³/4 cup sugar
1 teaspoon vanilla
 extract
1 cup all-purpose flour
³/4 cup chopped
 walnuts or pecans

1. Preheat oven to
moderate 350°F. Brush
8 inch square cake pan
with oil or melted butter;
line base with waxed
paper. Place chocolate
and butter in a medium
heatproof bowl over
simmering water. Stir
until melted and smooth.
Remove from heat, cool.
2. Stir in eggs, sugar and
vanilla. Add sifted flour
and nuts, combine well
(do not overbeat).
3. Pour mixture into
pan. Bake for 20–25
minutes or until skewer
comes out clean when
inserted in center. Cool
in pan; cut into squares.
Dust with combined
cocoa and confectioners'
sugar and top with
pecans, if you like.

Chocolate Brownies (top) and Panforte

Lemon Curd Tartlets

Preparation time:
  40 minutes +
  standing
Total cooking time:
  15 minutes
Makes 20

1 cup all-purpose flour
2 oz chilled butter,
  chopped
2 egg yolks
1/4 cup sugar
1–2 teaspoons grated
  lemon rind
1 tablespoon lemon
  juice

Filling
1/2 cup sugar
2/3 cup fresh lemon
  juice, strained
2 tablespoons thick
  cream or 2 oz butter,
  extra
3 eggs
2 egg yolks, extra

1. Place flour in food
processor. Add butter,
process 15–20 seconds
until mixture resembles
fine bread crumbs. Add
yolks, sugar, rind and
juice. Process for
20–30 seconds until
mixture just comes
together. Turn onto a
floured surface and
knead gently into a
ball. Wrap in plastic
wrap and refrigerate
for 45–60 minutes.
2. Roll pastry out

thinly on a lightly
floured surface, or
between two sheets of
waxed paper. Cut into
circles using a round
2 1/2–2 3/4 inch cutter.
Brush pastry circles
with a little oil or
melted butter and press
gently into muffin top
pans; prick all over
with a fine skewer or
fork. Place in freezer
for 30 minutes or
longer before baking.
3. Preheat oven to
moderate 350°F. Cut
sheets of waxed paper
large enough to cover
each pastry circle.
Spread a layer of dried
beans or rice evenly
over paper. Bake for
10 minutes, or until
golden and crisp.
Remove paper and
beans or rice.
4. **To make Filling:**
Whisk sugar with
lemon juice in a
medium bowl. Whisk
in cream or butter, eggs
and yolks. Mix well.
Transfer mixture to
medium pan. Whisk
over medium heat for
4 minutes, or until the
mixture is thickened
and smooth. Spoon
evenly into pastry
shells, leaving a small
edge of pastry. Bake
tartlets for another
8–10 minutes. Cool,
then transfer to a wire
rack. Decorate tartlets
with whipped cream
and candied peel, if
you like.

Fig and Nut Roll

Preparation time:
  20 minutes
Total cooking time:
  40 minutes
*Makes 1 large or 2
small rolls*

1 cup soft pitted dried
  figs, or dried dates,
  chopped
3/4 cup light brown sugar
1 teaspoon baking soda
2 oz butter, chopped
1–2 teaspoons grated
  orange rind
1 cup boiling water
2 cups self-rising flour
1/4 teaspoon ground
  nutmeg
1/4 teaspoon ground
  cinnamon
1/4 teaspoon ground
  allspice
1/4 teaspoon ground
  ginger
1 egg
1 teaspoon vanilla extract
1 cup pecans, toasted
  and chopped

1. Place figs or dates,
sugar, soda, butter and
rind in a large bowl.
Pour boiling water
over. Stir together until
butter and sugar are
melted. Allow to cool.
2. Preheat oven to
moderate 350°F. Brush
lids and sides of two
8 x 3 inch bread molds
with melted butter.
Leave a 2 inch collar of
waxed paper above
edge of each mold.

Lemon Curd Tartlets (top) and Fig and Nut Roll

3. Sift flour and spices together. In a small bowl, whisk egg with vanilla. Using a large metal spoon, fold flour and pecans alternately with egg into cooled cake mixture. Stir until smooth.
4. Spoon batter into molds. Bake with molds upright on a baking sheet in center of oven for 35–40 minutes or until a skewer comes out clean when inserted in center; the top should spring back when pressed with a finger. Cool in molds 5 minutes before turning onto wire rack to cool. Serve roll sliced, spread with butter.

Note: Bread molds are shaped tin canisters with lids on both ends and can be found in specialty kitchen stores or catalogues. To prevent crumbling, cool the roll before slicing.

13

Dark Carrot Cake with Rich Cream Cheese Frosting

Preparation time:
  30 minutes
Total cooking time:
  1 hour 20 minutes
Makes one 9¹/2 inch round cake

2 cups self-rising flour
2 teaspoons ground
  cinnamon
1 teaspoon ground
  cloves
1 teaspoon ground
  ginger
2 teaspoons baking
  soda
1 cup oil
1 cup light brown sugar
4 eggs
¹/2 cup golden syrup or
  dark corn syrup
11 oz grated carrot

Cream Cheese Frosting
8 oz cream cheese
2 oz butter, softened
1 cup confectioners'
  sugar
1 teaspoon vanilla
  extract or lemon juice
1 teaspoon grated
  lemon rind

1. Preheat oven to moderate 350°F. Brush a 9¹/2 inch deep, round springform cake pan with melted butter; line base and sides with waxed paper. Sift together flour, spices and baking soda.

2. Place oil, sugar, eggs and syrup in food processor. Add flour and spices and process 20–30 seconds. Add carrot and process again until well combined. Pour the mixture into prepared pan; smooth surface. Bake for 30 minutes. Reduce heat to moderately slow 315°F and cook for another 40–50 minutes, or until a skewer comes out clean when inserted in center of cake. Leave the cake in the pan for 10 minutes before turning onto a wire rack to cool.

3. When cake is cool, cut horizontally into two layers. Place base layer on a board or plate and spread with half the Cream Cheese Frosting. Replace top layer and spread remaining frosting over top of cake. Decorate cake with carrot curls and chopped walnuts, if you like. For best results, serve cake the next day.

4. *To make Cream Cheese Frosting:* Beat cream cheese with electric beaters in a medium bowl until smooth. Add butter, confectioners' sugar, vanilla or juice, and rind; beat together until mixture is light and creamy.

Chocolate-coated Coconut Macaroons

Preparation time:
  20 minutes
Total cooking time:
  20 minutes
Makes 25

2 egg whites
³/4 cup sugar
1¹/2 cups shredded
  coconut
6¹/2 oz dark chocolate,
  melted

1. Preheat oven to slow 300°F. Line two baking sheets with waxed paper. Beat egg whites in bowl until firm peaks form. Add sugar gradually, beating well after each addition and until sugar has dissolved and mixture is thick and glossy.

2. Transfer to larger bowl, add coconut. With a metal spoon, fold gently until ingredients are just combined. Drop level tablespoons of mixture onto baking sheets, about 1¹/4 inches apart. Bake 20 minutes or until lightly golden.

3. Cool completely on wire rack. Dip bases in melted chocolate and allow to set.

---

*Dark Carrot Cake with Rich Cream Cheese
Frosting (top) and Chocolate-coated
Coconut Macaroons*

Citrus Dried Fruit Delights

Preparation time:
  15 minutes
Total cooking time:
  20 minutes
Makes 18 pieces

1 *cup self-rising flour*
1 *teaspoon cinnamon*
³/4 *cup sugar*
¹/2 *cup golden raisins*
¹/4 *cup dried apricots,*
  chopped
¹/4 *cup dried pears,*
  chopped
¹/4 *cup dried apples,*
  chopped
2 *eggs, lightly beaten*
3 *oz butter, melted*

Lemon Glacé Icing
1 *cup confectioners'*
  sugar
¹/2 *oz unsalted butter,*
  melted
3–4 *teaspoons lemon*
  juice

1. Preheat oven to moderate 350°F. Brush an 8 inch square cake pan with oil or melted butter. Line base with waxed paper; grease the paper.
2. Sift flour, cinnamon and sugar into a bowl. Add golden raisins and dried fruit, stir. Make a well in the center.
3. Add combined eggs and butter. Mix well until smooth; do not overbeat. Pour into

prepared pan, smooth surface. Bake for 20 minutes or until a skewer comes out clean when inserted in the center. Leave cake in pan for 5 minutes before turning onto a wire rack to cool.
4. Cut into bars and spread with Lemon Glacé Icing. Decorate with chopped dried apricot, if you like.
5. *To Make Lemon Glacé Icing:* In a small bowl, combine sifted confectioners' sugar, melted butter, and enough lemon juice to form a firm paste. Stand bowl over pan of simmering water, stirring until icing is smooth and glossy—do not overbeat or icing will become dull and grainy. Remove from heat; spread over each piece of Fruit Delight, using a flat-bladed knife.

Note: Citrus Dried Fruit Delights can be stored in an airtight container for up to five days. They will keep, un-iced, in the freezer for up to three months.

Rich Prune and Apricot Cakes

Preparation time:
  30 minutes
Total cooking time:
  50-60 minutes
Makes two oblong cakes

¹/2 *cup currants*
8 *oz pitted prunes,*
  chopped
3¹/2 *oz dried apricots,*
  halved
¹/3 *cup mincemeat*
¹/2 *cup mixed dried fruits*
¹/4 *cup brandy*
5 *oz butter*
¹/4 *cup light brown sugar*
¹/4 *cup molasses*
2 *tablespoons barley*
  malt
2 *eggs*
¹/3 *cup self-rising flour*
²/3 *cup all-purpose flour*
¹/4 *teaspoon baking soda*
1 *teaspoon pumpkin pie*
  spice

1. Preheat oven to slow 300°F. Brush two 10¹/2 x 3 x 2 inch loaf pans with oil or melted butter. Line base and sides with waxed paper, extending paper ¹/2–³/4 inch above edge of pan on all sides. Combine currants, prunes, apricots, mincemeat, mixed fruits and brandy in medium pan. Stir over medium heat until all brandy has been absorbed. Remove from heat, cool slightly.
2. Beat butter and sugar

Rich Prune and Apricot Cakes (top) and Citrus Dried Fruit Delights

with electric beaters in small mixing bowl until light and creamy. Add molasses and malt and beat until ingredients are well combined. Add eggs gradually, beating well after each addition. Transfer to a large mixing bowl. Using a metal spoon, gradually fold in the sifted flours, baking soda and spice. Stir until smooth. Add the fruit mixture and stir until well combined.

3. Spoon mixture evenly into pans; smooth the surface. Tap the pans gently on bench to remove excess air bubbles from the mixture. Stand the pans on a baking sheet and bake for 50–55 minutes or until a skewer comes out clean when inserted into the center of the cakes. Leave cakes in the pans for 30 minutes before turning them onto a wire rack to cool. When the cakes are cool, dust the tops with sifted confectioners' sugar.

17

Chocolate Chip Peanut Cookies

Preparation time:
  15 minutes
Total cooking time:
  20 minutes
Makes 30

4 oz butter
1/2 cup sugar
1/4 cup light brown
  sugar, firmly packed
1 egg
1 cup self-rising flour
1/2 cup all-purpose
  flour
3/4 cup unsalted roasted
  peanuts
3/4 cup dark chocolate
  chips

1. Preheat oven to moderate 350°F. Line two 13 x 11 inch cookie sheets with waxed paper. Using electric beaters, beat butter and sugars until light and fluffy. Add the egg and beat thoroughly.
2. Transfer to a large mixing bowl; add sifted flours, peanuts, and chocolate chips. Using a large metal spoon, stir until ingredients are just combined and the mixture is smooth.
3. Knead the mixture lightly to form a soft dough. Roll one level tablespoon at a time into a ball.
4. Arrange on baking sheets, allowing room for spreading. Flatten gently with fingers. Bake for 15–20 minutes, or until golden. Remove cookies from oven, cool on sheets for 5 minutes before transferring to wire rack to cool.

Jam and Cream Sponge Cake

Preparation time:
  20 minutes
Total cooking time:
  25 minutes
Makes one 8 inch cake

3 eggs
1/3 cup sugar
1 teaspoon vanilla
  extract
1–2 teaspoons grated
  lemon or orange rind
1/2 cup self-rising flour,
  sifted
1 1/2 oz butter, melted
1 1/4 cups thick or
  pouring cream
1–2 tablespoons
  confectioners' sugar
1/3 cup strawberry or
  raspberry jam or
  lemon butter
sifted confectioners'
  sugar

1. Preheat oven to moderate 350°F. Brush two 6 3/4 inch shallow round cake pans with oil or melted butter; line base with waxed paper. Dust base and sides of pan with flour; shake out excess.
2. Place eggs and sugar into large heatproof bowl. Stand bowl over a pan of simmering water. Using hand-held electric beater or wire whisk, whisk until thick and pale yellow in color. Remove bowl from heat. Add vanilla and rind and beat for another 7–10 minutes, until lifted beater leaves a ribbon on the surface. Using a metal spoon, lightly fold in flour, incorporating as much air as possible. Fold in melted butter (mixture will deflate). Pour batter evenly into prepared pans, gently smooth surface.
3. Bake 20–25 minutes or until the top of the cake springs back when pressed with finger. Allow to cool in pan for 5 minutes before turning onto wire rack to cool completely.
4. Beat cream and confectioners' sugar until mixture holds firm peaks. Place one cake on board or plate. Spread with jam or lemon butter and then cream. Top with remaining cake. Dust top with sifted confectioners' sugar and decorate sponge with a strawberry, if you like.

*Jam and Cream Sponge Cake (top)
and Chocolate Chip Peanut Cookies*

Anzac Cookies

Preparation time:
  15 minutes
Total cooking time:
  20 minutes
Makes 28

1 cup all-purpose flour
3/4 cup sugar
1 cup rolled oats
3/4 cup shredded
  coconut
4 oz unsalted butter
2 tablespoons golden
  syrup or dark corn
  syrup
1/2 teaspoon baking
  soda
1 tablespoon boiling
  water

1. Preheat oven to
moderate 350°F. Line
two 13 x 11 inch cookie
sheets with waxed paper.
Sift flour into a large
mixing bowl. Add sugar,
oats, and coconut; make
a well in the center.
2. Combine butter and
syrup in small pan. Stir
over low heat until butter
has melted and mixture
is smooth; remove from
heat. Dissolve baking
soda in water; add to
butter mixture—it will
foam up instantly. Add
butter mixture to dry
ingredients. Using a
wooden spoon, stir
well until combined.
3. Shape one level
tablespoon of mixture
at a time into a ball,
place on prepared

baking sheets. Flatten
gently with fingers,
allowing room for
spreading. Bake for
15–20 minutes, or
until just brown.
4. Remove cookies
from oven and transfer
to a wire rack to cool.

Strawberry Coconut Slice

Preparation time:
  30 minutes
Total cooking time:
  40 minutes
Makes 18 pieces

4 oz butter
1/4 cup custard powder
3/4 cup all-purpose
  flour
1/3 cup sugar
1 egg, lightly beaten
3/4 cup strawberry jam

Topping
2 eggs, separated
1/3 cup sugar
1 teaspoon vanilla
  extract
3 cups shredded coconut

1. Preheat oven to
moderate 350°F. Brush
the base and sides of an
8 x 12 inch shallow
oblong pan with melted

butter or oil. Line base
with waxed paper.
2. Place butter, custard
powder, flour and sugar
in a medium mixing
bowl. Rub butter into
dry ingredients until
it resembles coarse
bread crumbs. Add
egg and mix to form
a smooth paste.
3. Spread mixture
evenly over base of
prepared pan. Bake in
preheated oven for
20 minutes, or until
firm and golden. Cool.
Spread base with
warmed jam.
4. *To make Topping:*
Using electric beaters,
beat egg whites in a
small bowl until stiff
peaks form. Add sugar
gradually, beating well
after each addition.
Transfer mixture to
large bowl. Add egg
yolks and extract.
Add coconut and stir
through gently and
lightly. Spread topping
over slice. Bake for
another 15–20 minutes
or until golden. Allow
slice to cool completely
before cutting into
squares with a
long-bladed, sharp
knife. Slice will keep
for up to three days in
an airtight container.

Note: Slice may be
made using jams such
as apricot, blackberry
or raspberry.

Anzac Cookies (top) and Strawberry Coconut Slice

Honey Nut Joys

Preparation time:
  30 minutes
Total cooking time:
  15 minutes
Makes 24 cookies

4 cups corn flakes
3¹/2 oz butter
¹/4 cup sugar
2 tablespoons honey
¹/2 cup crushed nuts
2 tablespoons sesame
  seeds, toasted

1. Preheat oven to moderate 350°F. Place paper liners in two 12-cup muffin pans.
2. Place the corn flakes in a large bowl. Combine the butter, sugar and honey in a small pan. Stir over medium heat without boiling until the sugar has dissolved. Bring to the boil, then remove from heat.
3. Pour the mixture over the corn flakes; add the crushed nuts and sesame seeds. Stir quickly until all ingredients are well combined and corn flakes are coated with syrup.
4. Place spoonfuls of the corn flake mixture evenly into the prepared pans. Bake for 10 minutes, or until Honey Nut Joys are just golden and slightly crisp. Leave to stand for 10 minutes in pans before transferring to a wire rack to cool.

Note: Store in an airtight container in a cool, dry place for up to a week.

Caramel Slice

Preparation time:
  15 minutes
Total cooking time:
  30 minutes
Makes 30

3/4 cup shredded
  coconut
1/3 cup light brown sugar
3/4 cup self-rising flour
3¹/2 oz butter, melted
1 teaspoon vanilla
  extract

Topping
13 oz sweetened
  condensed milk
1 oz butter
2 tablespoons golden
  syrup or dark corn
  syrup
2 teaspoons instant
  coffee
2 teaspoons hot water

Icing
4 oz dark chocolate,
  chopped
2 oz butter, chopped

1. Preheat oven to 350°F. Line base and sides of deep 11 x 7 inch rectangular pan with waxed paper, extending over all sides of the pan.
2. Place the coconut, sugar and flour in a large bowl and mix together. Make a well in the center. Stir in melted butter and vanilla; mix well. Press mixture evenly into base of prepared pan. Bake 12–15 minutes; remove slice from the oven before the edges begin to brown.
3. *To make Topping:* Place condensed milk, butter, syrup, and combined coffee and water in a small pan. Stir over medium heat until mixture boils. Reduce heat and simmer, stirring, for another 5 minutes. Pour caramel mixture over cooked slice base. Return baking sheet to oven and bake slice for another 10 minutes. Remove from oven and set aside to cool in pan.
4. *To make Icing:* Place the chocolate and butter in a small, heatproof bowl. Stand the bowl over a pan of simmering water. Stir until chocolate and butter have melted and the mixture is smooth. Spread icing evenly over the still-warm caramel layer of slice;

Caramel Slice (top) and Honey Nut Joys

smooth icing using a flat-bladed knife. Refrigerate Caramel Slice until icing sets.

Cut into squares or bars. Lift carefully from pan, removing corner slice first.

Note: Store Caramel Slice in an airtight container in a cool place for up to a week.

23

Jams, Preserves & Condiments

There is something luxurious about these hand-made gourmet delights in bottles and jars. Whether you make them as gifts or for a bake sale, they will be so much more appreciated than their commercial equivalents.

Kumquats in Liqueur

Preparation time:
  15 minutes
Total cooking time:
  50 minutes
Makes about 3 cups

1 lb kumquats
1 cup sugar
3/4 cup water
1/4 cup orange-flavored
  liqueur

1. Cut a cross in the top of each kumquat; pack into heatproof, sterilized jars.
2. Combine sugar and water in small heavy-based pan. Bring to boil, then boil for 1 minute. Stir in liqueur.
3. Pour syrup over kumquats, leaving 1/2 inch at the top of jars. Screw lids on loosely.

4. Place layers of newspaper on bottom of a large, heavy-based pan. Place jars on top and cover with enough hot water to reach top of jar rims.
5. Bring water slowly to simmer. Reduce heat slightly then simmer jars for 20 minutes, or until the kumquats start to look clear.
6. Remove jars carefully. Immediately tighten lids fully and cool completely. Label and date jars. Store in a cool, dark place for 2 months, turning jars upside down every couple of weeks.

> HINT
> Kumquats will develop more flavor the longer they are left to mature. Serve with a spoonful of syrup.

Chili Oil (left) and Kumquats in Liqueur

Chili Oil

Preparation time:
  10 minutes
Total cooking time:
  5 minutes +
  2 days standing
Makes 2¹/2 cups

2¹/2 cups vegetable oil
3 fresh whole chilies
1 cinnamon stick
2 teaspoons black
  peppercorns
fresh, whole pieces of
  chosen flavorings—
  herbs or whole spices

1. Heat the oil in a
large heavy-based
pan. Add the chilies,
cinnamon stick and
peppercorns. Remove
from heat then cover
and leave to stand for
2–3 days.
2. Strain the oil into a
sterilized bottle. Add
fresh, whole flavorings
to bottle.
3. Seal and label. Store
in a cool, dark place.

HINT
Fresh herbs such as
rosemary, basil, sage
or lemon grass may
be substituted for
the chilies.

Lemon Butter

Preparation time:
  10 minutes
Total cooking time:
  20 minutes
Makes about 1³/4 cups

4 eggs, lightly beaten
³/4 cup sugar
¹/2 cup lemon juice
2 teaspoons finely
  grated lemon rind
4 oz unsalted butter,
  chopped

1. Place eggs and sugar
in a large heatproof
bowl. Place bowl over a
pan of simmering water
and stir constantly with
a wire whisk until sugar
has dissolved.
2. Add the lemon juice,
grated rind and butter;
whisk until mixture is
smooth and butter has
melted. Beat constantly
with a wooden spoon
over barely simmering
water for about 20
minutes, or until the
mixture thickens and
coats the back of a
spoon. Remove from
heat immediately. (Do
not allow mixture to
boil or it will curdle.)
3. Pour or ladle warm
lemon butter into hot,
sterilized jars and seal
immediately. Allow to
cool completely before
labeling and storing in
a cool, dark place.

Easy Strawberry Jam

Preparation time:
  10 minutes +
  standing
Total cooking time:
  20 minutes
Makes 1¹/2 cups

1 lb ripe strawberries,
  washed and hulled
2 cups sugar
2 tablespoons lemon
  juice

1. Combine the
strawberries and sugar
in a medium heavy-
based pan. Allow to
stand for 10 minutes.
2. Add lemon juice
to the pan. Stir gently
over low to medium
heat, without boiling,
until sugar has
completely dissolved.
Bring slowly to the
boil, reduce heat and
simmer on high heat
for 35 minutes, or until
jam gels when tested.
3. Remove jam from
heat and allow bubbles
to subside. Set aside
for 2 minutes. Ladle
the hot mixture into
hot, sterilized jars
and seal the jars
immediately. Label and
date jars when cool.
Store in a cool, dark
place. Refrigerate jam
after opening.

Lemon Butter and Easy Strawberry Jam

Rich Mint Jelly

Preparation time:
  20 minutes +
  overnight standing
Total cooking time:
  40 minutes
Makes about 3 1/2 cups

2 lb green apples
4 cups water
1/2 cup lemon juice
2 1/2 cups mint leaves
sugar
*1/2 cup extra mint
  leaves, finely chopped*
*2–3 drops green food
  coloring*

1. Wash and cut apples into thick slices but do not peel or core.
2. Combine apple, water, juice and mint leaves in a large heavy-based pan; bring to boil. Reduce heat slightly and cook, uncovered, for 10–15 minutes or until apple forms a soft pulp. Break up any large pieces with a wooden spoon.
3. Strain mixture through muslin into a bowl—do not press liquid through muslin or it will become cloudy. Leave overnight. Measure the strained juice and return it to pan. Add 1 cup of sugar for each cup of liquid. Stir over low heat without boiling until sugar has dissolved completely. Bring to boil, reduce heat slightly; boil on low heat for about 20 minutes, or until mixture gels when tested.
4. Add extra mint and coloring, stir well until no streaking is visible and mint is distributed evenly. Remove from heat, set aside 5 minutes. Pour into hot, sterilized jars, seal immediately. Label and date the jars when cool. Store mint jelly in a cool, dark place for up to 12 months.

Rich Mint Jelly

1. Cut the washed apples into thick slices; do not peel or core.

2. Break up any large pieces of cooked apple with a wooden spoon.

3. Strain the mixture through a piece of muslin into a bowl.

4. Add extra mint and green food coloring to mixture, stirring well.

Fig and Spice Jam

Preparation time:
10 minutes +
overnight standing
Total cooking time:
35 minutes
Makes 4 cups

1 lb dried dessert figs
4 cups water
1/3 cup lemon juice
3 cups sugar, warmed
1/4 cup glacé ginger,
  chopped
2 teaspoons finely
  grated lemon rind
1 teaspoon whole
  cloves

1. Chop figs finely and place in medium bowl. Cover with the water and leave overnight.
2. The next day, transfer the figs and water to a large heavy-based pan. Bring to the boil, then reduce heat, cover and simmer for 10–15 minutes or until the figs become tender and plump.
3. Add the lemon juice, sugar, ginger, rind and cloves. Stir constantly over low heat until sugar has completely dissolved. Bring to the boil, reduce heat slightly and boil for 15–20 minutes, or until the mixture gels when tested; stir occasionally with a wooden spoon. Stir the mixture more frequently towards the end of cooking to make sure it does not catch or burn.
4. Remove jam from heat and set aside for 2 minutes. Using a heatproof jug, pour the jam into hot, sterilized jars and seal them immediately. Label and date the jars when cool.

Note: Fig and Spice Jam will keep in a cool, dark place for up to 12 months.

Pears in Rum

Preparation time:
20 minutes
Total cooking time:
20 minutes
Makes about 8 halves

1 lb small pears
1 1/2 cups sugar
1 cup water
2 cinnamon sticks
1/4 cup dark rum

1. Wash the pears, then peel and core. Place in a large bowl and cover with water. Set aside.
2. Place sugar and water in a medium heavy-based pan. Stir over low heat, without boiling, until sugar has completely dissolved. Brush sugar crystals from sides of pan with a wet pastry brush. Bring to boil, reduce heat slightly and boil syrup for 10 minutes without stirring.
3. Drain water from pears. Place pears and cinnamon sticks into a pan with syrup and simmer for another 5–6 minutes, or until the pears are tender. Carefully turn the fruit several times during cooking to coat with syrup. Remove pears from syrup and pack into sterilized jars.
4. Add rum to the syrup and return to heat. Bring to boil and boil for 2–3 minutes. Gently pour the syrup over the fruit in jars and seal. Set aside for 2–3 days, to allow flavor to penetrate fruit, before serving.

HINT
Pears in Rum make a delicious summer dessert, served with ice-cream. In winter they can be heated and served with thick cream, or with a creamy custard sauce.

Pears in Rum (top) and Fig and Spice Jam

Dried Fruit Chutney

Preparation time:
  15 minutes
Total cooking time:
  30 minutes
Makes 3 cups

3 large green apples
*1/2 cup pitted prunes,
  chopped*
1/2 cup dates, chopped
*1/2 cup dried apricots,
  chopped*
1/4 cup lemon juice
3/4 cup brown sugar
1 cup malt vinegar
1/2 cup water
1/2 teaspoon nutmeg

1. Peel, core and chop apples. Place all ingredients in a medium, heavy-based pan. Stir over medium heat until sugar has dissolved.
2. Increase heat to high and bring mixture to the boil. Reduce heat slightly and boil for 25–30 minutes, or until the chutney has thickened. Stir the mixture occasionally.
3. Remove chutney from heat and set aside for 5 minutes. Using a heatproof jug, pour mixture into hot, sterilized jars. Seal immediately. When cool, label and date jars. Store in a cool, dark place for up to 12 months.

Prunes in Rum

Preparation time:
  10 minutes + 1 week
  standing
Total cooking time:
  5 minutes
Makes 4 cups

1 1/2 lb pitted prunes
3/4 cup dark rum
*1/4 cup light brown
  sugar, lightly packed*
2 cinnamon sticks
*rind of 1 lemon, cut
  into thick strips*
2 cups water
3 whole cloves

1. Place prunes in a medium bowl. Place remaining ingredients in pan. Bring to boil. Remove from heat.
2. Pour syrup over prunes. Allow to cool completely and place in warm, sterilized jars, covering prunes completely with syrup. Seal jars, label and date.
3. Store in a cool dark place for 1 week before using. Refrigerate after opening—will keep for up to 12 months.

Herb Vinegar

Preparation time:
  10 minutes
Total cooking time:
  5 minutes +
  2 days standing
Makes 2 1/2 cups

1 lemon
2 1/2 cups white vinegar
2 bay leaves
1 piece rosemary
*2 tablespoons fresh
  oregano, chopped
  sprigs of fresh herbs
  or fresh whole spices,
  for flavoring*

1. Peel lemon, using a vegetable peeler, into thick strips. Remove any white pith with a sharp knife. Heat the vinegar in a small pan until simmering. Remove from heat, add flavorings.
2. Cover and allow to stand for 2 days, stirring occasionally.
3. Strain vinegar into a sterilized bottle. Add fresh flavorings.
4. Seal tightly. Label bottle and store in a cool place. Herb Vinegar will keep well for up to six months.

Note: This vinegar has a rich herb and citrus flavor and is ideal for dressing salads.

---

*Clockwise from top left: Herb Vinegar, Dried Fruit
Chutney and Prunes in Rum*

Citrus Trio Marmalade

Preparation time:
  40 minutes + 20
  minutes standing
Total cooking time:
  1 hour 10 minutes
Makes 4 cups

2 grapefruit
3 limes
2 oranges
4¹/2 cups water
3³/4 cups sugar,
  warmed

1. Peel long strips of rind from grapefruit, limes and oranges, using a vegetable peeler; remove and retain any thick white pith. Slice rind into thin strips, using a sharp knife.
2. Squeeze juice from fruit, reserve juice. Place the seeds, pith, and flesh onto a piece of muslin and tie muslin with string.
3. Place the peel, juice, water and muslin bag in a large heavy-based pan. Bring to the boil, reduce heat and simmer, uncovered, for 45–50 minutes, or until contents of pan have reduced by half. Remove muslin bag, squeezing out excess juices. Add sugar to pan, stir until sugar has dissolved. Bring to the boil; boil steadily, uncovered, on low heat 15–20 minutes, or until a spoonful of mixture placed on a cold plate wrinkles when pushed with a finger.
4. Allow marmalade to stand 20 minutes. Skim gently if necessary. Pour into hot, sterilized jars; seal immediately. Label and date when cool.

Note: Blood oranges are delicious in this recipe.

Citrus Trio Marmalade

1. Remove and reserve thick white pith from grapefruit, lime and orange rind.

2. Place the muslin bag containing seeds, pith and flesh into the pan.

3. Place a spoonful of mixture on a cold plate and push with your finger to test.

4. Leave marmalade to stand for 20 minutes, skimming gently if necessary.

Whisky Mincemeat

Preparation time:
20 minutes +
overnight standing
+ 2 weeks standing
Total cooking time:
Nil
Makes 4 cups

1 *large green apple,*
  peeled and grated
1 *cup golden raisins*
1 *cup raisins, finely*
  chopped
1 *cup currants*
1/2 *cup mixed candied*
  citrus peel
2 *tablespoons glacé*
  ginger, finely chopped
rind and juice of
  1 *lemon*
rind and juice of
  1 *orange*
1/3 *cup blanched*
  almonds, chopped
2 *teaspoons pumpkin*
  pie spice
1/2 *cup light brown*
  sugar, lightly packed
1/4 *cup whisky*
1 3/4 *oz butter, melted*

1. Place all ingredients
in a large, non-metal
mixing bowl. Stir until
thoroughly combined.
Cover, leave overnight.
2. Spoon into warm,
sterilized jars, seal at
once, label and date.
Leave 1–2 weeks before
using. Store mincemeat
in a cool, dark place
for up to 12 months.

HINT
Use mincemeat as a
filling for fruit tarts,
or decorate jars
with pretty ribbon
and fabric to make
holiday gifts.

Mustard Pickles

Preparation time:
  15 minutes +
  overnight standing
Total cooking time:
  10–12 minutes
Makes about 4 cups

3 *medium cucumbers,*
  chopped
1 *large onion, chopped*
6 1/2 *oz cauliflower, cut*
  into tiny florets
1 *large green bell*
  pepper, chopped
2 *tablespoons salt*
2 *teaspoons brown*
  mustard seeds
2 *tablespoons mustard*
  powder
1/2 *teaspoon turmeric*
  powder
1 *bay leaf*
1 *cup malt vinegar*
1/4 *cup sugar*
1 *tablespoon*
  cornstarch
2 *tablespoons water*

---

1. Combine the
cucumbers, onion,
cauliflower, and bell
pepper in a large
non-metal bowl.
Sprinkle vegetables
with salt and leave to
stand overnight.
2. Wash and drain
the vegetables, rinsing
thoroughly to remove
all salt. Place in a large
heavy-based pan. Add
the mustard seeds,
mustard powder,
turmeric, bay leaf,
vinegar and sugar. Stir
over low heat until
mixture boils. Simmer,
uncovered, for
8–10 minutes, or until
vegetables are tender.
3. Combine the
cornstarch and water
in a small mixing
bowl. Add mixture
to the pan and stir
through the vegetables
quickly. Bring to the
boil, then remove from
heat once the mixture
has thickened.
4. Spoon pickles into
hot, sterilized jars and
seal immediately. When
the jars have cooled,
label and date.

Note: Most types of
pickling vegetables are
suitable for use in this
recipe. The selection
above will give a good
combination of
flavors and textures,
but experiment with
others if you prefer.

Mustard Pickles (top) and Whisky Mincemeat

WHISKEY MINCE MEAT

Green Tomato Chutney

Preparation time:
20 minutes
Total cooking time:
1–1 1/2 hours
Makes about 5 cups

3 lb green tomatoes,
chopped
2 small green apples,
peeled and chopped
1 large onion, chopped
1 teaspoon salt
1/2 cup golden raisins
1 teaspoon whole black
peppercorns
1 tablespoon brown
mustard seeds
2 cups light brown
sugar, lightly packed
2 cups white vinegar
1/2 teaspoon sweet
paprika

1. Place all ingredients in a large, heavy-based pan. Stir over low heat until sugar has dissolved.
2. Increase heat to medium and bring mixture to the boil. Simmer, uncovered, for 1–1 1/2 hours, or until chutney has thickened. Stir mixture occasionally. Stir more frequently towards the end of cooking time to ensure mixture does not catch or burn.

3. Remove from heat, set aside for 5 minutes. Pour mixture into hot, sterilized jars; seal immediately. Label and date when cool. Store in a cool, dark place for up to 12 months.

Note: Cooking time will vary depending on ripeness of tomatoes.

Sweet Rich Chili Sauce

Preparation time:
20 minutes
Total cooking time:
35 minutes
Makes 3 cups

8–10 ripe egg or
plum tomatoes,
chopped
2 large green apples,
chopped
1/2 cup dates, chopped
1/2 cup raisins
1/2 cup golden raisins
1 cup white vinegar
1 teaspoon ground
cinnamon
1 teaspoon ground
paprika
2–3 fresh chilies,
chopped
1/2 cup light brown
sugar, lightly packed

1. Combine all the ingredients except the sugar in a medium heavy-based pan. Stir until all ingredients are thoroughly combined. Bring to the boil, reduce heat slightly and boil for 20 minutes, or until mixture is thick and pulpy.
2. Remove sauce from heat. Push the mixture through a sieve and return to the pan. Add sugar and stir over medium heat until it has dissolved. Return to boil and simmer for another 10–15 minutes or until the sauce has thickened.
3. Use a heatproof jug to pour the sauce into hot, sterilized jars or bottles. Seal at once and leave to cool. Label and date the bottles.

Note: Sweet Rich Chili Sauce may be bottled without sieving if a thicker, chunkier version is preferred.

> **HINT**
> This sauce is delicious served either hot or cold. The amount of chili can be varied according to taste. The recipe above is for a very mild sauce; for a hotter version, increase the number of chilies.

Green Tomato Chutney (top) and Sweet Rich Chili Sauce

Quick and Easy Plum Sauce

Preparation time:
15 minutes
Total cooking time:
35 minutes
Makes about 1¹/2 cups

1 teaspoon whole
cloves
1 cinnamon stick
1 bay leaf
1 teaspoon whole black
peppercorns
1 teaspoon brown
mustard seeds
1 lb 11 oz can dark
plums, drained and
chopped
1 medium onion, finely
chopped
¹/2 cup light brown
sugar, lightly packed
1¹/2 cup malt vinegar

1. Place cloves, cinnamon stick, bay leaf, peppercorns and mustard seeds on a small, square piece of muslin. Secure with a piece of string.
2. Place plums, onion, sugar and vinegar in a large, heavy-based pan. Stir over low heat until sugar has dissolved.
3. Place muslin bag in pan. Increase heat to medium and bring to the boil; reduce heat slightly and boil for 30–35 minutes or until sauce has thickened.
4. Remove from heat and cool slightly. Place mixture in food processor and press the pulse button for 20 seconds, or until sauce is smooth and free of large chunks.
5. Pour sauce into hot sterilized bottles or jars and seal immediately. Label and date when cool. Store in the refrigerator for up to six months.

Apricot and Ginger Jam

Preparation time:
15 minutes +
overnight standing
Total cooking time:
1 hour
Makes 4 cups

1 lb dried apricots
5 cups water
6¹/2 oz preserved ginger
in syrup, thinly sliced
3³/4 cups sugar, warmed
2 tablespoons lemon
juice
¹/2 cup slivered almonds

1. Place whole apricots in a medium bowl, cover with water and soak overnight.
2. Transfer apricots and water to a large heavy-based pan. Bring to boil, reduce heat, cover and simmer 15 minutes or until apricots are tender.
3. Add ginger, sugar, and juice to pan. Stir constantly over low heat until the sugar has dissolved. Bring to the boil, reduce heat slightly and boil, uncovered, for 25–30 minutes or until mixture gels.
4. Remove from heat and allow to stand for 2 minutes. Add the almonds and stir. Spoon into hot, sterilized jars and seal immediately. Label and date jars when cool.

Figs in Whisky

Preparation time:
10 minutes
Total cooking time:
35 minutes
Makes about 3 cups

1 lb dried figs
1¹/2 cups strong cold tea
¹/2 cup whisky or dark
rum
1 cinnamon stick
¹/4 cup light brown
sugar, firmly packed
1 lemon
1 orange

1. Place the figs, tea, whisky and cinnamon stick in a large heavy-based pan. Slowly bring to boil. Reduce heat, simmer 25–30 minutes, or until figs are tender and plump.
2. Stir in sugar. Peel lemon and orange, using a vegetable peeler. Remove any thick white

From top: Figs in Whisky, Quick and Easy Plum Sauce, Apricot and Ginger Jam

pith and cut peel into thin strips with a sharp knife. Add to the pan. Simmer for another 5 minutes.

3. Juice the lemon and the orange. Add juice to pan. Remove cinnamon stick. Pour mixture into hot,

sterilized jars; seal immediately. Label and date when cool. Store in a cool, dark place for up to 12 months.

Toffee & Candies

Luscious, hand-made candies like these are simply irresistible. Tie them up in pretty bundles, or arrange in small presentation boxes. They will add a touch of class to your fete, and they make exquisite gifts.

Buttered Brazil Nuts

Preparation time:
  10 minutes
Total cooking time:
  20 minutes
Makes 24

2 cups sugar
$^1/2$ cup water
2 tablespoons golden syrup or dark corn syrup
4 oz unsalted butter
1 tablespoon white vinegar
2 cups whole brazil nuts

1. Line two 13 x 11 inch baking sheets with waxed paper.
2. Combine sugar, water, syrup, butter and vinegar in a medium, heavy-based pan. Stir over medium heat, without boiling until butter has melted and sugar has dissolved. Brush sugar crystals from the sides of the pan with a wet pastry brush. Bring to the boil, reduce heat slightly, then boil without stirring for about 20 minutes; or boil until a teaspoon of the mixture dropped into cold water reaches soft-crack stage. If a sugar thermometer is used, the mixture must reach 275°F. Remove from heat immediately.
3. Using a wooden spoon, dip each whole nut into the butterscotch mixture. Place onto prepared baking sheets to set. Store between sheets of waxed paper in an airtight container at room temperature for up to 7 days.

Note: Other varieties of nuts can be used instead of brazil nuts.

Chocolate Nut Surprises (left) and Buttered Brazil Nuts

Chocolate Nut Suprises

Preparation time:
  20 minutes
Total cooking time:
  20 minutes
Makes about 50

3¹/2 oz hazelnuts
3¹/2 oz cashew nuts
3¹/2 oz almonds
8 oz dark chocolate,
  chopped
2 oz milk chocolate,
  melted

1. Line a 13 x 11 inch cookie sheet with waxed paper or foil. Grease paper or foil with oil or melted butter. Preheat oven to moderate 350°F. Place nuts on baking sheet. Bake in preheated oven for 10 minutes or until golden. Cool on baking sheet.
2. Place dark chocolate in small, heatproof bowl. Stand bowl over pan of simmering water and stir until chocolate is melted and smooth. Remove from heat.
3. Sandwich together one of each nut with a little melted chocolate; allow to set. Dip nut clusters into melted chocolate to completely coat; remove with a fork, drain excess chocolate and place nuts on prepared baking

sheet. Allow to set.
4. Pipe or drizzle milk chocolate over nut clusters in a zig-zag pattern. Store clusters in airtight container in a cool, dark place, or in the refrigerator during hot or humid weather.

Chocolate Cherry Cups

Preparation time:
  20 minutes
Total cooking time:
  5 minutes
Makes about 50

8 oz dark good quality
  chocolate, melted
50 foil candy cases

Filling
3¹/2 oz dark chocolate,
  roughly chopped
¹/2 cup thick or pouring
  cream
2 tablespoons coffee
  liqueur
3¹/2 oz glacé cherries,
  quartered

1. Pour a teaspoonful of melted chocolate into each candy case. Use a small brush to coat inside of case thickly with chocolate, leaving no gaps.
2. Turn cups upside-down on a wire rack to set. Spoon remaining chocolate into a small paper decorating bag and pipe patterns onto

a sheet of waxed paper or foil. Allow to set.
3. **To make Filling:** Place chocolate in small heatproof bowl. Stand bowl over a pan of simmering water, stir until chocolate has melted. Add cream and liqueur; stir until smooth.
4. Place a piece of cherry into each cup. Spoon filling into each cup up to the rim. Tap gently to release any air bubbles. Place a piped pattern on top of each chocolate. Store in a cool, dark place for up to two weeks.

Molasses Caramel Toffees

Preparation time:
  40 minutes
Total cooking time:
  15–20 minutes
Makes 80

3/4 cup turbinado sugar
1/4 cup molasses
3¹/2 oz butter
1/2 cup condensed milk

1. Line base and sides of shallow 8 x 12 inch oblong cake pan with foil, leaving edges overhanging. Brush the foil with melted butter or oil.
2. Combine all ingredients in a medium, heavy-based pan. Stir

Molasses Caramel Toffees (top) and Chocolate Cherry Cups

over medium heat without boiling until sugar has completely dissolved. Bring to boil then reduce heat slightly. Stir constantly for 15–20 minutes, until the mixture turns a dark caramel color.

3. Pour mixture into pan; smooth surface. Mark into squares with a sharp, flat-bladed knife. Leave on a wire rack to cool. When toffee has completely set, break into squares.

Note: Store in airtight container in a cool, dry place for up to three weeks. Refrigerate in warmer weather.

45

Mixed Chocolate Truffles

Preparation time:
  15 minutes
Total cooking time:
  5 minutes
Makes 30

6¹/2 oz dark chocolate,
  roughly chopped
1 oz butter
2 tablespoons heavy
  cream
1¹/2 cups crushed
  chocolate wafer
  cookies
2–3 teaspoons dark
  rum
2–3 teaspoons Kirsch
3¹/2 oz dark chocolate,
  grated
3¹/2 oz white chocolate,
  grated

1. Melt chocolate, butter and cream in a small pan over low heat, stirring until chocolate has melted and mixture is smooth.
2. Add crushed wafers and stir gently to combine. Divide mixture into two bowls. Add rum to one bowl and Kirsch to the other and mix each well. Refrigerate for 5–10 minutes, or until mixtures are firm enough to shape.
3. Shape balls from each mixture, using 2 level teaspoons for each ball. Roll rum truffles in grated dark chocolate and Kirsch truffles in grated white chocolate. To store, place in candy cases between sheets of waxed paper in an airtight container. Store in refrigerator for up to two weeks.

Note: Truffles may be rolled in combined grated chocolate and sifted cocoa powder.

Golden Honeycomb

Preparation time:
  10 minutes +
  1¹/2 hours setting
Total cooking time:
  20 minutes
Makes about 28 pieces

1¹/2 cups sugar
¹/4 cup light corn syrup
1 tablespoon golden
  syrup or dark corn
  syrup
¹/2 cup water
2 teaspoons baking soda

1. Line base and sides of an 11 x 7 inch oblong pan with foil. Brush foil with melted butter or oil.
2. Combine sugar, syrups and water in a large, heavy-based pan. Stir over medium heat without boiling until sugar has completely dissolved. Brush sugar crystals from sides of pan with a wet pastry brush. Bring to boil, reduce heat to medium and boil without stirring for 6–8 minutes or until mixture just starts to turn a deep golden color (about 300°F on a sugar thermometer). Remove from heat immediately.
3. Add baking soda quickly to sugar mixture. Using a wooden spoon, stir gently until mixture bubbles and increases in volume and no baking soda is visible on the surface. Over-stirring will cause the mixture to deflate.
4. Pour gently into pan and leave to set for 1¹/2 hours. Remove from pan, peel away foil and break into pieces. Store honeycomb in an airtight container between layers of waxed paper.

HINT
Honeycomb pieces can be dipped into melted chocolate. Decorate with piped melted chocolate, if you like.

---

*Golden Honeycomb (top) and
Mixed Chocolate Truffles*

Rose Turkish Delight

Preparation time:
20 minutes
Total cooking time:
20 minutes
Makes 36 pieces

1 1/4 cups boiling water
rind of 1 orange
rind of 1 lemon
2 tablespoons gelatin
2 cups sugar
1/4 cup orange juice
2 tablespoons rosewater
red food coloring
3/4 cup confectioners'
  sugar, sifted

1. Rinse an 8 inch square cake pan with water; line base with waxed paper. Place half the water and the rind in a medium pan. Bring to boil, reduce heat and simmer for 10 minutes.
2. Combine gelatin and remaining water in a small bowl. Stir with a fork until gelatin has completely dissolved.
3. Add sugar, gelatin mixture, juice and rosewater to the pan. Reduce heat and stir until sugar dissolves. Bring to boil, then boil on low heat 10 minutes. Remove from heat. Add a few drops of food coloring. Mix well.
4. Strain mixture into wetted pan. Allow to cool and set overnight at room temperature. Dust confectioners' sugar over a piece of waxed paper. Turn out Turkish Delight onto confectioners' sugar and cut into 36 pieces using a flat-bladed knife dipped in confectioners' sugar. Dust pieces with more sugar. Refrigerate in an airtight container for up to one month.

Note: Buy rosewater in well-stocked supermarkets, or in Middle Eastern stores.

Chocolate Caramel Fudge

Preparation time:
20 minutes
Total cooking time:
20 minutes
Makes 36

2 cups sugar
1 cup milk
2/3 cup heavy cream
1/4 cup light corn syrup
1 teaspoon vanilla
  extract
2 3/4 oz dark cooking
  chocolate, chopped

1. Line base and sides of a deep 8 inch square cake pan with foil. Brush foil with melted butter or oil.
2. Combine sugar, milk, cream and corn syrup in a large, heavy-based pan. Stir over medium heat without boiling until sugar has completely dissolved. Brush sugar crystals from side of pan with a wet pastry brush. Bring to boil, reduce heat slightly and boil without stirring for 15 minutes; or boil until a teaspoon of mixture dropped into cold water reaches soft ball stage. If using a sugar thermometer, mixture must reach 245°F. Remove from heat immediately.
3. Cool mixture for 5 minutes. Add vanilla; beat vigorously with a wooden spoon for 5 minutes or until mixture begins to thicken and lose its gloss. Pour into pan; smooth surface. Leave on wire rack to cool.
4. Place chocolate in a small heatproof bowl. Place over a pan of simmering water, stir until chocolate has melted and is smooth. Cool slightly. Spread chocolate evenly over fudge, using a flat-bladed knife. Leave to set. When firm, remove from pan. Carefully peel off foil and cut into squares. Store in an airtight container in a cool, dark place for up to two weeks.

Rose Turkish Delight (top) and
Chocolate Caramel Fudge

Hard Caramels

Preparation time:
  15 minutes
Total cooking time:
  15 minutes
Makes 49 pieces

1 cup sugar
3 oz butter
2 tablespoons golden
  syrup or dark corn
  syrup
1/3 cup light corn syrup
1/2 cup condensed milk
8 oz dark chocolate,
  chopped

1. Brush base and sides of an 8 inch square cake pan with melted butter or oil. Line base and sides with waxed paper; grease paper. Combine sugar, butter, syrups and condensed milk in medium heavy-based pan. Stir over medium heat without boiling until butter has melted and sugar has dissolved completely.

Brush sugar crystals from the sides of pan with a wet pastry brush.
2. Bring to boil, reduce heat slightly and boil, stirring, for about 10–15 minutes, or until a teaspoon of mixture dropped into cold water reaches hard ball stage. If using a sugar thermometer, mixture must reach 250°F.
3. Remove from heat immediately. Pour into prepared pan and leave to cool. While caramel is still warm, mark squares with an oiled knife; when cold, cut into squares.
4. Line two 13 x 11 inch baking sheets with aluminum foil. Place chocolate in a small heatproof bowl. Stand bowl over a pan of simmering water, stir until smooth. Remove from heat, cool slightly. Using two forks, dip caramels one at a time

into the chocolate to coat. Lift out, drain excess chocolate, then place on prepared baking sheets. Leave to set. Store hard caramels in an airtight container in a cool, dark place for up to four weeks.

> **HINT**
> If you prefer, the chocolate coating can be omitted and the chocolate simply piped or drizzled on top of the caramels. In warm weather, use good quality chocolate—it will set faster at room temperature and is usually easier to work with.

Hard Caramels

1. Remove sugar crystals from the side of the pan with a wet pastry brush.

2. Boil mixture until a teaspoonful forms a hard ball when dropped in cold water.

3. *Mark mixture into squares with an oiled knife while still warm.*

4. *Dip caramels one at a time in melted chocolate, using forks.*

Just for Kids

Colorful, fun to make and delicious to eat, these novelty treats are bound to capture the imagination of the young. They're sure to be top sellers at the bake sale, and make great kids' party food as well.

Cat & Mice Cakes

Preparation time:
40 minutes
Total cooking time:
20 minutes
Makes 12

4 oz butter
1 teaspoon finely grated
orange rind
3/4 cup sugar
2 eggs, lightly beaten
2 cups self-rising flour
1/2 cup milk

Frosting
4 oz butter
2 cups confectioners'
sugar, sifted
2 tablespoons milk
food coloring
assorted candies for
decorating

1. Preheat oven to moderate 350°F. Brush two 6-cup, 1/2-cup capacity muffin pans with melted butter or oil. Using electric beaters, beat butter, rind and sugar in small mixing bowl until light and creamy. Add eggs gradually, beating well after each addition.
2. Transfer to a large bowl. Using a large metal spoon, fold in the sifted flour alternately with milk. Stir until just combined and mixture is smooth.
3. Spoon into prepared muffin pans, filling two-thirds of each cup. Bake for 20 minutes, or until cakes are lightly golden. Turn onto wire rack to cool. Spread top of each cooled cake with frosting and decorate with candies to make faces.
4. To make Frosting: Using electric beaters, beat butter in small mixing bowl until light and fluffy. Add sifted confectioners' sugar and milk and beat until mixture is smooth. Tint portions of icing in different colors.

Cat and Mice Cakes and Crackajack

Crackajack

Preparation time:
  10 minutes
Total cooking time:
  30 minutes
Makes 9 cups

2 tablespoons oil
1/3 cup popping corn
3/4 cup light brown
  sugar
3 oz butter
1/4 cup light corn syrup
1/4 teaspoon baking soda
1/4 teaspoon vanilla
  extract
1 cup roasted salted
  peanuts
3/4 cup golden raisins

1. Preheat oven to moderate 350°F. Line a 13 x 11 inch baking sheet with foil. Heat oil over low heat in a medium, heavy-based pan. Scatter corn over base of pan in a single layer. Put a tight-fitting lid on pan and allow corn to pop. (This should take no longer than 4 minutes.) When corn has stopped popping, remove from heat; turn popcorn onto foil-lined baking sheet to cool.
2. Combine the sugar, butter and syrup in small heavy-based pan. Stir gently over low heat for 5 minutes, or until sugar has dissolved. Attach a sugar thermometer to the side of the pan. Simmer, uncovered, for 5 minutes or until the thermometer reads 250°F (hard-ball stage); stir occasionally.
3. Remove the pan from heat and remove the thermometer from pan. Stir baking soda and vanilla into caramel mixture. Pour over the popcorn, stirring to coat. Bake 5 minutes, stir popcorn, then bake for another 5 minutes. Remove popcorn from oven, add peanuts and golden raisins; cool.
4. Break Crackajack into pieces. Store in an airtight container in a cool place.

Creepy Crawlies

Preparation time:
  25 minutes
Total cooking time:
  55–60 minutes
Makes 25

4 egg whites
1 cup sugar
green and red food
  coloring
licorice and assorted
  candies for decorating

1. Preheat oven to very slow 250°F. Brush two baking sheets with melted butter or oil and line with waxed paper. Place egg whites in a large, dry bowl. Using electric beaters, beat until soft peaks form.

2. Add sugar gradually, beating constantly until mixture is thick and glossy, and sugar has dissolved. Divide the meringue mixture in half. Add a few drops of green food coloring to one bowl and a few drops of red to the other and beat until combined.
3. Spoon each meringue mixture into a separate decorating bag, each fitted with a 1/2 inch plain, round tip. Pipe caterpillar shapes about 3–4 inches long with the green meringue, onto prepared baking sheets; pipe snail shapes with the pink meringue. Decorate snails and caterpillars with assorted candies to form features. Bake for 55–60 minutes or until meringues are crisp. Turn off the oven but leave the meringues inside until they have completely cooled. Remove Creepy Crawlies from the oven and store carefully in an airtight container.

HINT
Caterpillars and snails can be tinted any color. Use various candies for features— tiny chocolate chips, or gumdrops halved, for eyes; cut up gummi worms for mouths; licorice sticks for antennae.

Creepy Crawlies

1. Cut each slice of cake into three circles, avoiding brown edge.

2. Using reserved butter mixture, attach chocolate button halves to each cake.

Green Frogs

Preparation time:
55 minutes
Total cooking time:
Nil
Makes 9

14 oz purchased
    pound cake
3¹/2 oz butter
²/3 cup confectioners'
    sugar, sifted
2 teaspoons milk
red food coloring
vanilla or raspberry
    extract
9 chocolate buttons,
    halved
assorted candies
    (licorice allsorts)

Icing

3 cups confectioners'
    sugar
5 tablespoons boiling
    water
2 teaspoons gelatin
green powder, paste or
    liquid food coloring

1. Cut pound cake into three pieces lengthways. Cut each slice into three circles, avoiding dark brown layer on outside of cake, using a 2¹/2 inch plain round cutter.

2. Beat butter in a medium bowl with electric beaters until smooth. Add confectioners' sugar and milk, continue beating until mixture is light and creamy. Tint with red food coloring until pale pink and flavor with extract; mix well. Spread small mounds of mixture evenly on top of each cake circle, reserving about 1 tablespoon of mixture. Trim edges of cake, tapering diagonally from top, with a sharp knife. Attach chocolate button halves to sides of cakes with reserved butter mixture. Place cakes on a baking sheet and refrigerate for 2–3 hours or until firm.

To make Icing: Sift confectioners' sugar into a large bowl. Make a well in the center. Place 2 tablespoons of the water in a small bowl. Sprinkle gelatin on top; stir gently until dissolved. Add mixture to remaining water. Pour onto confectioners' sugar and stir until the mixture is smooth and free of lumps. Tint with green food coloring; mix well.

3. Place one cake on the flat part of a fork. Spoon icing over cake, allowing excess to drain back into the bowl (make sure all sides are well covered). Transfer to a wire rack, using a knife to carefully ease cake off the fork.

4. Decorate frogs with candies for eyes and feet. Carefully cut out mouths with a sharp, pointed knife. Allow to set completely.

Green Frogs

3. *Holding cake on the flat part of a fork, spoon icing over.*

4. *Decorate frogs with candies to make eyes and feet.*

Creamy Coconut Ice

Preparation time:
  20 minutes + 1 hour
  refrigeration
Total cooking time:
  Nil
Makes 30 pieces

2 cups confectioners'
  sugar
$1/4$ teaspoon cream
  of tartar
13 oz can condensed
  milk
$3^1/2$ cups shredded
  coconut
2–3 drops pink food
  coloring

1. Brush an 8 inch square cake pan with oil or melted butter. Line base with waxed paper.
2. Sift the confectioners' sugar and cream of tartar into a large bowl. Make a well in the center and add condensed milk. Stir in half the coconut; add the remaining coconut. Using your hands, mix until well combined.
3. Divide mixture in half. Tint one half with pink food coloring. Using your hand, knead color through evenly.
4. Press pink mixture over the base of prepared pan; cover with the white

mixture and press down firmly to even the surface. Refrigerate for 1 hour or until firm. Remove Coconut Ice from pan and cut into squares or bars. Store in an airtight container in a cool, dark place for two to three weeks.

Toffee Apples

Preparation time:
  10 minutes
Total cooking time:
  20 minutes
Makes 12

12 small red or green
  apples, very crisp
4 cups sugar
2 cups water
2 tablespoons white
  vinegar
red or green food
  coloring

1. Line two 13 x 11 inch baking sheets with foil. Brush foil lightly with oil or melted butter.
2. Wipe apples well with a clean, dry towel. Push a wooden ice-cream bar stick or a thick skewer firmly into the stem end of each apple.

3. Combine sugar, water, and vinegar in a large, heavy-based pan. Stir over medium heat without boiling until sugar has completely dissolved. Brush sugar crystals from sides of pan with a wet pastry brush. Add food coloring. Bring to the boil, reduce heat slightly, then boil without stirring for about 15 minutes, or boil until a teaspoon of the mixture dropped into cold water reaches small-crack stage. If using a sugar thermometer it must reach 275°F. Remove from heat immediately.
4. Dip apples, one at a time, into syrup to coat. Lift out and twist quickly to coat evenly. Drain, then place each apple on prepared baking sheets. Leave to set at room temperature. When set, wrap each toffee apple in cellophane and tie with ribbon. Toffee apples can be kept for up to two days.

> HINT
> It is important that apples are at room temperature when they are dipped into hot toffee. If they are too cold, the toffee will form bubbles on the surface.

Toffee Apples (top) and Creamy Coconut Ice

Marzipan Mice

Preparation time:
  20 minutes +
  refrigeration + 2 days
  drying
Total cooking time:
  Nil
Makes 16

6¹/2 oz almond meal or
  very finely ground
  almonds
1 cup confectioners'
  sugar, sifted
1 egg white
almond extract, optional
32 colored sugar balls
16 currants
colored curling ribbon

1. Combine almonds and confectioners' sugar in a medium bowl. Make a well in center. Add egg white, using a wooden spoon, and stir until well combined. Add extract, if using. Turn onto work surface and knead for 5 minutes until fairly dry and smooth. Cover with plastic wrap, refrigerate for 10 minutes.

2. Divide marzipan into 16 equal portions. Mold by rolling into a round. Remove two small pieces for the ears. Roll remaining marzipan into a log shape, tapering the front to make the face. Place two sugar balls in place to form the eyes.

3. Make two small incisions above the eyes for the ears. Roll out remaining reserved marzipan and press into the holes to form the ears. Press a currant in position to form a nose.

4. Make another incision in the rear of the mouse and insert a colored piece of ribbon to match the eye color. Allow to dry out for two days. Store in an airtight container in the refrigerator for up to four weeks.

Marzipan Mice

1. Add egg white to almonds and confectioners' sugar, using a wooden spoon.

2. Taper the front of a long piece of marzipan to make mouse face.

3. Press reserved marzipan into holes above the eyes to form ears.

4. Place a colored piece of ribbon in rear end of mouse to form tail.

Rainbow Popcorn

Preparation time:
  10 minutes
Total cooking time:
  15 minutes
Makes about 4 cups

2 tablespoons oil
1/2 cup popping corn
1 1/2 cups sugar
1 3/4 oz butter
1/2 cup water
2–3 drops red food
  coloring
2–3 drops green food
  coloring
2–3 drops yellow food
  coloring

1. Preheat oven to moderate 350°F. Heat oil in a large pan. Add corn, cover and cook over medium heat. Hold lid tightly, shake pan occasionally. Cook until the popping stops, then set aside.
2. Combine sugar, butter, and water in a small, heavy-based pan. Stir over medium heat until the sugar has dissolved. Brush sugar crystals from sides of pan using a wet pastry brush. Bring to the boil; boil without stirring for 5 minutes.
3. Remove from heat. Divide syrup into three equal portions and place in small bowls. Add coloring to each bowl; stir until combined and no streaking is visible. Divide popcorn into three equal portions. Toss each colored syrup through a batch of popcorn until pocorn is well coated.
4. Place popcorn onto a baking sheet and bake for 5 minutes or until popcorn has separated and crystallized. Place popcorn in a large bowl, toss to combine colors. Serve on the day of making, or keep for up to two days in an airtight container.

Cone Suprises

Preparation time:
  20 minutes +
  overnight setting
Total cooking time:
  20 minutes
Makes 20

1 cup sugar
1/4 cup water
3 teaspoons gelatin
1 tablespoon boiling
  water
3 egg whites
20 small round or
  square colored
  ice-cream cones
assorted candies
  for decoration
1/4 cup sprinkles

1. Combine sugar and water in a medium, heavy-based pan. Stir over low heat without boiling until sugar has completely dissolved. Bring to boil, reduce heat to low. Simmer for 4 minutes. Combine gelatin and boiling water in a small bowl. Stir until gelatin is dissolved. Add to sugar syrup in pan. Simmer for another minute.
2. Beat egg whites in a large bowl until stiff peaks form. Gradually beat in hot syrup in a thin stream. Continue beating 10–15 minutes or until thick and glossy and cooled; the mixture should have the right consistency for a decorating bag and hold its shape.
3. Place ice-cream cones on a baking sheet. Fill bases with assorted candies. Spoon mixture into a decorating bag fitted with a 1/2 inch round, fluted tip. Pipe large swirls of marshmallow into each cone. Spread sprinkles on piece of waxed paper and lightly dip each marshmallow peak to coat half of peak. Place a piece of licorice or a candy on the other side. Allow to set overnight. Cones may be stored in an airtight container for up to two days.

Rainbow Popcorn (top) and Cone Surprises

Index

Front cover, top row: Herb Vinegar (page 32), Caramel Slice (page 22), Toffee Apples (page 59), Citrus Trio Marmalade (page 34), Creamy Coconut Ice (page 59), Lemon Curd Tartlets (page 12), Buttered Brazil Nuts (page 42)